The Official

Dog Codependents Handbook

The Official

Dog Codependents Handbook

For People Who Love Their Dogs Too Much

by

Ronnie Sellers

Illustrated by Jennifer Black Reinhardt

Published by Ronnie Sellers Productions, Inc.

Acknowledgements

The author would like to acknowledge the following dogs for the
contributions they made to the publication of this book . . .

Cindy

Karl

Barney

Jenny

MIck

Lucille

Lily

and Lola

Dedications

This book is fondly dedicated to those of you who have written to me to
confess the many ways in which you
love your dogs too much.

Ronnie Sellers

To those with and without fur who have given me love.

Jennifer Black Reinhardt

Author's Note

Four years ago the first edition of *The Official Dog Codependents Calendar* was published. On the back page of this calendar (and in subsequent editions), I invited people to write to *Dog Codependents Anonymous*, care of our editorial office, to tell us their dog stories.

Since then I have collected hundreds of letters. The letters come from people from all walks of life: housewives and school teachers, lawyers and sociologists, psychologists and veterinarians, and even children. Some of the letters are only one paragraph long. Others go on for ten pages. Most of them are intended to be funny, but often I wonder whether I should be laughing in response to what I'm reading...or crying.

The letters have one thing in common. They were all written by people who love their dogs very much.

I have included some of these letters, or excerpts from them, in this book to help illustrate the various aspects of Dog Codependency and to prove that my observations about Dog Codependents are not merely figments of my imagination.

I promised the authors of these letters that I would respect their privacy. I have, therefore, included only their initials and their home towns with their letters. If you think you recognize someone whose letter is included here, please don't phone or write me for verification. I am sworn to secrecy. I shall carry the secret confessions of the Dog Codependents who confide in me with me to my grave.

And if you do recognize respondents, please don't use their admissions about their Dog Codependence against them. After all, it seems that most of us are addicted to something these days. One could do a lot worse than to choose a dog.

Table of Contents

X

Introduction

There are people in this world, many people as it turns out, who love their pets too much. I first realized this during an autographing session I was doing in New England. I was in a bookstore signing one of my children's books when a woman approached me and asked me if I would sign twelve books, one for each of her cats. As I signed books for Muffy and Felix and Chezzy and Romeo and Tigger, the woman went on to explain how she had "story hour" for her "babies" every evening after supper. She sat in a large over-stuffed chair with her cats all around her and read to them from picture books. At Christmas it was her custom to give each cat his or her own picture book, personally autographed by the author.

The table at which I was sitting happened to be in the self help section of the bookstore. As the woman expounded upon her relationships with her different cats I made a note in my journal; "There are people who are Cat Codependents: they love their cats too much!."

This journal entry became the seed idea for *The Official Cat Codependents Calendar*, which I published a year later. In each month of the calendar, which was illustrated by my friend Jennifer Black Reinhardt, I described a different characteristic of Cat Codependents.

The calendar struck a chord with cat lovers throughout North America. Over the next four years we sold more than a quarter of a million copies. As the number of calendars in circulation increased, so did my mail. I received letters from all over the world from people who had seen the calendars. These people all had one thing in common; they had very unusual stories to tell about their relationships with their pets.

At first, as might be expected, most of these letters came from cat fanciers. It wasn't long, however, before I began to receive mail from "the other half" as well—people whose lives revolved around their relationships with their dogs.

Why, they asked (often somewhat contentiously), hadn't I published a calendar for Dog Codependents as well? Did I have some sort of bias? Didn't I know that there are as many dog owners in this country as there are cat owners? "My Dobie and I want equal time," one respondent said succinctly. He didn't have to elaborate because he enclosed a photograph, one of those panoramic shots that's about seven inches wide. It was a closeup of his Doberman baring all of its teeth. In the margin below the photograph the owner had scribbled, "This isn't a smile. My dog and I know where you live."

"Never argue with a growling dog," my grandfather used to tell me. I decided to heed his advice and publish a Dog Codependents calendar, too.

After four years in print, it has sold almost 200,000 copies. I have received hundreds of letters from Dog Codependents since then. After reading them, I became convinced that Dog Codependency is a real condition with life-altering consequences.

"We are owned by three uniquely different miniature poodles, two chocolate and one vanilla" one couple from Houston, Texas, wrote. "They share our meals, our bed, our car, go on trips with us, even share our shower. We all do obedience training work, but they know who is really obeying whom."

Another writer confided, "All of the members of my family say that they want to be reincarnated as one of my dogs. Somehow I've accumulated four of them: two miscellaneous terriers, Saki (17 yrs) and Mikey (16 yrs), Bunky, a refugee from a puppy mill who was advertised in our local paper as an 'old one-eyed, two-toothed, shih-tzu' (how could I resist) and finally Hobo, our not-so-street-smart Lahsa Apso from the local pound. Taking one hyper and three blind dogs out for a walk resembles a Maypole dance. I am such a Dog Codependent that I have built a ramp up to my bed so my old dogs can still get up onto it to sleep."

A woman from Mableton, Georgia wrote and confessed that she was such a total Dog Codependent that she had spent two years "shopping for a new house that would be suitable for my 'boys' (my dogs). I drove several real estate agents to distraction taking the dogs around with me to examine the different places that were for sale. When I finally found the right house I waited another month after the closing to move in because the entire yard had to be fenced in and doggy doors installed. No way I'm gonna inconvenience my babies."

As much as I appreciated hearing from these Dog Codependents, I never anticipated the effect their stories would have on me. When I look back on it now, I realize that at first I was really reading their letters out of obligation. These were, after all, people who had purchased one of my calendars. They deserved to receive my attention and consideration.

But as the number of letters increased, I became aware of stirrings deep down within myself, vague feelings of uneasiness that I couldn't suppress. I began to have a recurring dream in which I threw a stick far out into a tranquil lake and then watched as a beautiful black dog swam out to retrieve it.

I found myself reading the Pets section of the classifieds almost obsessively. Every time I went past a pet supply store I felt an irrational yearning to go in and purchase a leash or a dog bone or a dog toy of some sort.

Were the letters from Dog Codependents getting under my skin? There was the obedience school dropout who felt an overwhelming sense of shame every time he saw another dog owner successfully command his dog to "heel." There was the young woman who quit a lucrative new job in Hattiesburg, Mississippi and moved back to Atlanta because her dog missed his friends back in the old neighborhood. There was the woman whose jealous German Shepherd had scared off five potential husbands before she could get them to the altar.

"Something's happening to me," I finally admitted to a friend. "When I first started reading these letters from Dog Codependents, I pitied them. I couldn't believe that anyone could ever let themselves get so absorbed in a relationship with a dog. Now, the more letters I read, the more I find myself almost envying them."

"Maybe you should pay attention to your feelings," the friend replied.

"What's that supposed to mean," I answered defensively.

"Well, what I mean is maybe there's something that you're hiding from, something about dogs that you've repressed."

"Who me!" I scoffed. "Don't be ridiculous. I don't even own a dog. I haven't owned a dog in...ten years."

The friend took off his eyeglasses and looked me directly in the eyes. "Maybe that's the problem," he said with a wry smile. I felt a tingling sensation at the base of my spine. Then the tingle ignited and sent a burst of heat up through my back and into my head. I felt dizzy. I began to perspire. I knew what this meant. It meant that the truth had just bitten me in the haunches.

∗　　　　　∗　　　　　∗

One of the happiest moments of my childhood was the day that my father came home from work with a very fuzzy, very wrinkled and very black Cocker Spaniel puppy. We named her Cindy, because she was as black as a cinder.

The saddest day of my childhood was the day my Father took Cindy to the animal shelter because she had nipped at one of my playmates. Although we'd had her for less than a year, I'd still become very attached to her. I begged my father to go back and reclaim Cindy. I vowed to watch her every minute of the day to make sure that she didn't nip at another child ever again.

My father would not be swayed. After a while I stopped trying to convince him. I knew it was hopeless. I cried hysterically for three nights straight. I was sure that I would die from sadness. It was my first experience with losing love.

I didn't die, but lived through it, and in so doing I learned a valuable lesson. I learned that life does go on and, in fact, things really do get better with time.

Things got much better because we got Karl, a 125 pound German Shepherd. Karl galloped tirelessly around the neighborhood with me in tow on my rollerskates. He pulled me up snowy hills on my sled in the winter. He protected me from the neighborhood bullies, and guarded our house against the meter readers, trash men and brush salesmen. In the mornings he lifted my bed up off of the floor as he attempted to get out from beneath it.

Karl stayed by my side constantly as I grew from a boy into a young man.

Barney was the homeless mongrel puppy that I adopted while in college. She (that's right, she...somehow "Barney" seemed to suit her better than any feminine name) followed me relentlessly through the streets of Philadelphia during a spring downpour until I ducked into the campus bookstore. When I came out an hour later, she was still sitting there waiting for me, soaked to the bone and shivering. I stopped and looked down at her. She looked up at me with doleful eyes. A drop of water fell from her nose onto my shoe. She looked down at the drop, then back up at me and wagged her tail ever so slightly, as if to apologize for getting my shoe wet. With that, she won my heart. I picked her up and wrapped her in my jacket and took her home with me on the subway. I spent the next three weeks nursing her back to health.

Then came Jenny, another abandoned (and emotionally stressed) puppy, followed by Mick, the contortionist Weimaraner who tied his legs up into knots each evening while he slept.

Lucille was the last. Another mutt...a German Shepherd-Labrador mix (like Barney). Lucille travelled all over the country with me while I worked in a band. I stashed her into my garment bag and snuck her into hotels. I taught her how to close the hotel doors that my fellow band members were forever leaving open. She guarded our bus each night while we were on stage. Lucille was the smartest of them all. She was also the most dependent, and that was her undoing.

I left her with a friend while I went home to visit my family during the holidays. Lucille's anxiety over my absence caused her to run away from the friend's house during a particularly severe New England snowstorm. She never came back and I never saw her again.

It took me years to stop missing Lucille. I looked for her every time a car went by with a dog in it. I drove through the neighborhood that she disappeared in time after time in hopes that I might find her. Somehow, when I finally accepted that Lucille was gone, I just couldn't bring myself to go out and get another dog. For ten years I remained "dogless."

My friend's suggestion that I reflect upon the role dogs had played in my life was the impetus that started me thinking about getting a dog again. Then came my kids. My son Lindsey was about to turn fourteen. My daughter Jaime was turning ten. After the divorce, they had to return each day after school to my empty house. "We need a dog, Dad," my son stated matter-of-factly. "This house needs more life in it."

I promised both of them that I would consider their request, but that I wouldn't agree to get a dog until summer arrived and my business travel was finished for the season. This was a terrific excuse. The truth was I wasn't ready to assume the responsibility of owning another dog yet. Summer arrived. My children reminded me of my promise. I stalled some more.

And then I began work on this book.

I hadn't written more than the first sentence when I suddenly stopped, pushed back my chair, put on my cap and got up to leave my office.

"I'm going to the animal shelter," I told our office manager.

"What for?" she asked incredulously.

"I think I need to get a dog," I said.

"Oh," she replied, and she stared at me quizzically as I walked out of the office and got into my car.

"I'll just have a look at the different dogs in the shelter," I said to myself. "Better to adopt a dog than to start from scratch with a new puppy. All those ruined shoes and messy carpets."

Walking through the shelter was almost maddening. More than forty dogs began barking simultaneously the moment I walked into the kennel area. Their shrill yelps echoed off of the cement walls and metal roof of the building. The dogs jumped and paced and panted and whined in a frenzy of anxiety.

I held my fingers in my ears and tried to focus on each dog as I passed by its kennel. An old Lab that was blind in one eye seemed terribly lonely. I paused for a moment, but kept going. It didn't feel right. A Pit Bull bounced up and down as if on a pogo stick and snapped its jaws and barked at the apex of each jump. Probably not a good choice given the fact that there were so many young kids in my neighborhood.

There were mongrels and purebreds; big dogs and small dogs; black, white, yellow and red dogs. I just couldn't seem to find one that I connected with.

I got all the way to the last row of kennels and leaned over to look at a coon hound. He had huge ears and seemed to be totally preoccupied with smelling things. He looked up at me suddenly and, startled, let out a loud, eerie, multi-pitched howl. "Sounds too much like a werewolf," I thought to myself.

I stood up and, feeling a bit disappointed, turned toward the exit. Just as I was about to leave, I looked down and noticed a medium-sized black dog staring up at me from her kennel. She didn't move. She didn't bark. She just looked me in the eyes. She was a Shepherd-Labrador mix…the *mirror image* of Lucille.

I reached through the cyclone fence with my hand and the dog licked it affectionately. She gave a few wags of her tail, then stopped and fixed my eyes with her stare. I knew that I'd found my dog.

I brought my children into the shelter to meet "Lola" later that afternoon. We had an intimate thirty minutes together in a large dog training room at the back of the shelter. Lola stood up on her hind legs and put her front paws on my daughter's shoulders and gave her a big smooch. My daughter was won over. Then Lola went and sat down in front of my son and offered him her paw as if she was closing the deal. He laughed and took her paw. We went out to the office and signed the adoption papers.

Lola has been with us now for almost a month. In that amount of time she has learned how to "fetch" and "sit" and "stay" and "lie down." She's working on "heel". She won't let me out of her sight. I don't like to let her out of mine.

They say that you should "write what you know." Now that Lola has come into my life, I realize I know a lot about Dog Codependency.

My friend was right. It was time for me to have a dog again. When you read what is contained in these pages, make no mistake. You are reading about me. I am a Dog Codependent. I will always be a Dog Codependent.

What's more, (like so many of the Dog Codependents who have written to me over the years), I wouldn't have it any other way.

The Official
Dog Codependents Handbook

Chapter 1
Symptoms of Dog Codependency

Dear Dog Codependents Anonymous,

At one time I traveled 32 weeks a year. When I got a new puppy I couldn't stand to leave him, so instead of flying like a sane person I bought a new van so Cutty could go too.

Well, he ate it!...along with 3 hotel rooms.

So I decided to buy Cutty a puppy as a play-mate. I had a huge separate area built at my friend's kennel and spent a fortune on a cedar-sided, glass windowed (screens of course) puppy palace for them while I was away.

Now I don't travel anymore and Cutty is gone, but I still have his puppy (JoJo), an English Mastiff (Rosy), and a boxer (Scotty). This is great, except my living room also has three pieces of furniture. At 160 lbs., Rosy fills the couch. At 80 lbs., Scotty prefers the chaise. My soft, comfy Italian chair is just the right size for JoJo (a petite Gordon Setter). I tell all my friends, "I'm a floor person, I never sit on furniture." The truth is there isn't any left. I finally decided to do something about it.

It was like shopping for the three bears. That night I had three plush dog beds lined up in front of the TV, one huge, one large and one normal sized.

The dogs looked. They sniffed. They climbed back up on their previous perches. I threw up my hands, curled up my body and, as I patted the biggest dog bed lying next to me, I said to my husband, "I hope you like yours too, honey!"

T.L.C.
Gold Hill, OR

3

A Dog Codependent's first thought in the morning is about the dog.

Dog Codependents Anonymous,

Since Topper was a puppy he would wake up and just stare at me if he wanted to go out. He never barked or said anything. He would always just be there, staring at me. When I would wake up and say "good morning," he would, quick as a flash, slip his long tongue in my mouth. I learned long ago to turn my head away as I spoke to him in the morning to avoid the tongue. I thought it was cute and never broke him of the habit.

Barkingly Yours,

RECEIVED
1/11

E.V.R. Jr.
Fishkill, NY

4

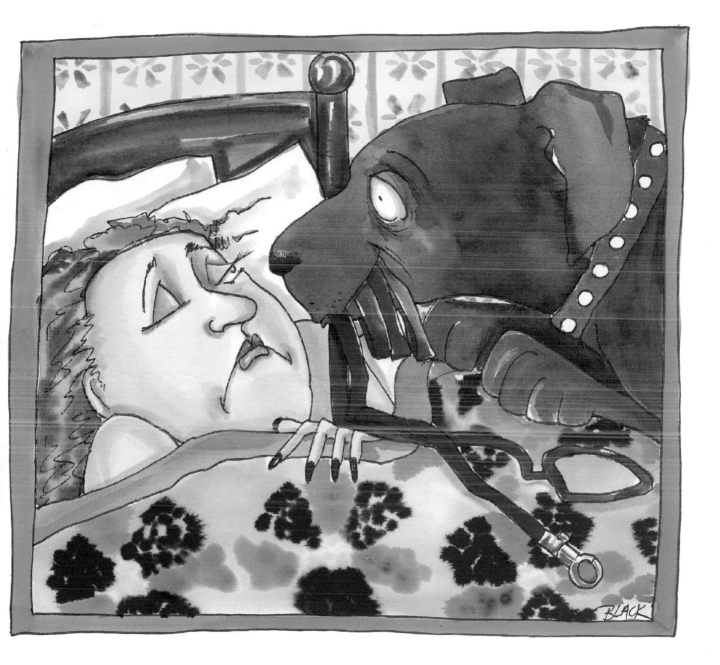

5

Dog Codependents are often the last to realize that they are powerless and their lives have become unmanageable.

Dear Dog Codependents Anonymous,

We recently received one of your calendars as a Christmas gift. It fits us perfectly. It's wonderful to know there are others out there whose lives revolve around their canine companions!

Our five "children," Too-Too, Luke, Max, Conan and Shane are our pride and joy. We recently purchased a large house and pickup truck with a cap – for the "kids."

I am sure glad to see that we're not the only crazy "parents" out there! Please put us on your mailing list – I don't think we can afford NOT to be members of DCA much longer.

H. and R.C.
West College Corner, IN

RECEIVED
2/13

Many Dog Codependents bear a
remarkable resemblance to their pets.

Quotations to Live by:

In order to really enjoy a dog, one doesn't try to train him to be
semi-human. The point of it is to open oneself to the possibility of
becoming partly a dog.
Edward Hoagland

He may look just the same as you,
    and he may be just as fine,
But the next-door dog is the next-door dog,
    and mine-is-mine.
Dixie Wilson

If you are a dog, and your owner suggests that you wear a sweater,
suggest that he wear a tail!
Fran Leibowitz

9

To Dog Codependents, every dog is a lap dog.

Dear Dog Codependents,

I have been Codependent over Old English Sheepdogs for 22 years now. Presently my life is run by two 3-year olds named "Windsor" and "Wellington."

One condition (the only one) that I placed upon my acceptance of my husband's marriage proposal was that he would buy me an Old English Sheepdog puppy as soon as I found one that I wanted.

We just celebrated our 22nd anniversary. As always, we went out to dinner to celebrate but brought home bread and crackers to share the joy with "our boys." We figure the joy they get from this sharing is worth at least 95% of the dinner cost, so we do it often. Ha!

Cheers,

Ms. J.J.
Austin, TX

RECEIVED
8/19

11

Leaving pooch at the kennel is a very traumatic experience for Dog Codependents.

Dear DCA,

How wonderful and relieving to read that I am not alone with my feelings for my dog! I rescued my Basset Hound, Sissy, from the local Humane Society and she has become the most wonderful "pain in my butt" ever since!

I tell people all the time that I wouldn't trade her for a million dollar lottery ticket and that I'll probably end up in therapy when she dies. They think I need therapy now!

J.S.W.
Tucson, AZ

RECEIVED
1/8

Dog Codependents have no reservations about smooching with pooch, even though they know full well where pooch's smoocher has been.

Greetings Dog Codependents,

My husband and I are proud to be owned and bossed by three wonderful canines: Sweetums, a 12-year old Beagle mix; Sugar Bear, a 4-year old Cocker Spaniel; and Sam, a small, blonde mutt (parentage and age unknown).

Here are more traits of dog codependence:

1. Dog Codependents order pizza because their dogs like the crusts.

2. Dog Codependents would never think of using their mate's toothbrush, but think nothing of kissing the dog on the lips.

Looking forward to hearing from you soon.

G.L.K.
Clermont, FL

RECEIVED
7/22

15

Dog Codependents will only patronize "dog friendly" resorts. After all, what fun would a holiday be without the dog? And besides, leaving pooch behind in some sort of dog kennel would be out of the question. The poor thing would be emotionally scarred for life by the experience.

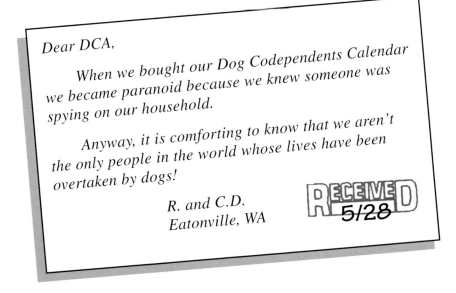

Dear DCA,

When we bought our Dog Codependents Calendar we became paranoid because we knew someone was spying on our household.

Anyway, it is comforting to know that we aren't the only people in the world whose lives have been overtaken by dogs!

R. and C.D.
Eatonville, WA

RECEIVED
5/28

Dog Codependents prefer to own convertibles.

Every Dog Codependent knows that the way to a dog's heart is through its stomach.

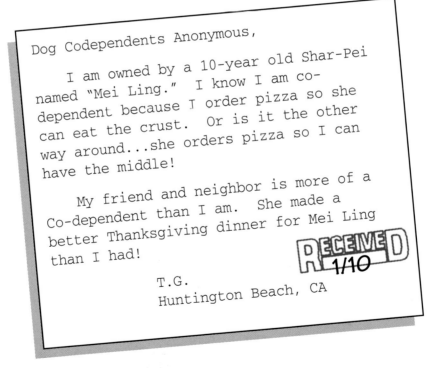

Dog Codependents Anonymous,

I am owned by a 10-year old Shar-Pei named "Mei Ling." I know I am co-dependent because I order pizza so she can eat the crust. Or is it the other way around...she orders pizza so I can have the middle!

My friend and neighbor is more of a Co-dependent than I am. She made a better Thanksgiving dinner for Mei Ling than I had!

RECEIVED 1/10

T.G.
Huntington Beach, CA

21

Chapter 2
The Causes of Dog Codependency

Dear Dog Codependent Friends,

In several of the groups that I belong to my name is no longer J_____, it is "the Dog Lady." I was even put in our church directory as The Dog Lady.

I live with two Giant Schnauzers, a Cairn Terrier and I was willed a Miniature Schnauzer.

As my father and I put the finishing touches on the waterbed we've built for my Schnauzers for Christmas, I must finally admit to my codependence.

Give me a baby to watch for five minutes and I'm a nervous wreck, but bring me ten dogs to watch for a week or so and I'm fine.

When my husband and I go out for pizza, our waitresses know to box the crust for the dogs.

Dog Codependent? I think I fit the mold.

J.H.
Belleville, IL

23

While there is little data to support the theory, many Dog Codependents believe their condition is hereditary...that there is some dog lover gene they inherited from their ancestors and will pass on to their children and grandchildren.

Sometimes Dog Codependency strikes
suddenly and without warning.

Dear Dog Codependents Anonymous,

My family presented me with this year's
calendar. They all agree that they want to
be reincarnated as one of my dogs. Somehow
I've accumulated four: two miscellaneous
terriers - Saki, (17 yr.) and Mickey, (16
yr.) Bunky, a refugee from a puppy mill and
advertised in our local paper as a "one-eyed,
two-toothed, Shih-tzu, old female (how could
I resist?) and finally Hobo, our
not-so-street-wise Lahsa Apso from the local
pound. Taking one hyper and three blind dogs
out for a walk resembles a Maypole dance. I
adore each one of them! Please mark me as
co-dependent first class on your mailing
list.

L.W.
New Westminster, BC

RECEIVED
2/8

Other times it is the result of years and years of spoiling the dog – frequently to a ridiculous extreme.

Dear DCA,

Please put me on your mailing list. I am chauffeur, maid, masseuse, groomer, playmate, nurse, cook, and exercise coach for three lovely Bernese Mountain Dogs that I adore.

I have completely "gone to the dogs" and I am enjoying every minute of it!

L.A.
Seekonk, MA

RECEIVED 1/23

Recent evidence seems to suggest that Dog Codependence is a highly contagious virus which is spread when a "carrier" comes into contact with others in a confined area.

31

Freudians believe that Dog Codependency
results from having an overbearing,
domineering dog during childhood.

Dear Dog Codependents Anonymous,

At long last — someone who will understand me!

I've been owned since age 7 by cocker spaniels
(I'm now 55). I can't imagine what my life
would have been like without Blondie, Holly,
Heidee, Randy, and Hersey.

Please add my name to your mailing list!

C.J.
Norton, MA

RECEIVED
12/21

Sleep deprivation is a tactic frequently used by dogs to gain control of their owners' minds and make them dependent.

Dear Dog Codependent Friends,

Please add me to your mailing list. I probably have one of the most severe cases of Dog Codependency ever known to man.

My 2$\frac{1}{2}$ year old 90 pound Doberman, Cole, is a big bed hog. He doesn't sleep at the bottom of the bed, either. He sleeps horizontally next to me with his head resting on a pillow. Also, he has to have his head stroked until he falls asleep at night. He may seem like he's just a big baby, but he's the best guard dog and companion I've ever had.

Cole's first home with me was directly behind the governor's mansion in Little Rock while Bill Clinton was governor. This means Cole may have political "pull." He used to go crazy barking at Socks whenever I took him on our daily walks. He just can't seem to get along with cats.

K.M.
Little Rock, AR

RECEIVED
7/29

35

Some believe that a dog's breath contains a powerful "nerve gas" which robs humans of their ability to reason and opens the door for mind control.

Top Ten Dogs Rated by Intelligence

1. Border Collie
2. Poodle
3. German Shepherd
4. Golden Retriever
5. Doberman Pinscher
6. Shetland Sheepdog
7. Labrador Retriever
8. Papillon
9. Rottweiler
10. Australian Cattle Dog

(Source: S. Cohen, The Intelligence of Dogs, The Free Press, 1993)

37

Some Dog Codependents believe their dogs are famous people reincarnated, and claim that they were brought together with their pets by karmic destiny.

Dear DCA,

I thought your readers would like to know that when Elvis died he came back as my dog, Mick.

S.H.F.
Bowling Green, KY

RECEIVED
6/4

(Editor's note: It's not that we don't believe *you*. It's just that we're not entirely convinced that Elvis is really dead. But that is the most original "Elvis Sighting" we've heard in a long time!)

39

Chapter 3

When Someone You Love Loves Dogs

Dear Dog Codependents Anonymous,

Please allow me to introduce you to my dear lady friend, Ms. L.L.M., the proud (and extremely codependent) owner of a year old Sheltie named "Peanut." Ms. M and "Nut" were thrust together shortly after the dog's birth, and it was and continues to be case of love to such an extreme that I have prayed that when I die, I come back as a dog.

Ms. M doesn't understand that Nut is a dog. She takes her to work with her and obediently walks her every three or four hours, feeds her special treats and basically does anything Nut (her daughter, she claims) wants.

Ms. M speaks four known dialects of Sheltie, including the difficult-to-master Southern Maryland variety.

Ms. M has a trailer full of Sheltie memorabilia. All her friends buy her Sheltie stuff as gifts. She misses the dog when they are, on rare occasions, apart and admits that she can't stand to be separated from it.

To say that the dog is spoiled is the understatement of the decade. Please enroll this woman in the DCA and send her all upcoming literature related to your organization.

I have personally never been much of a dog person, but in a short time I've grown to love the little mutt, too. Maybe you should enroll me in DCA too, before it's too late.

M.E.M.
Indian Head, MD

RECEIVED
6/28

41

It is not uncommon for Dog Codependents to have intimacy problems.

Dear Dog Codependents Anonymous,

My 110-lb. yellow Lab mix, Montana, is quite the bed hog. I don't mind, but my 6'8" husband is very possessive about his personal sleeping space! But how great on cold winter nights to have Montana under the covers with me (before hubby comes to bed) to warm me up with his radiating body heat!

Fondly,

L.R.C.
Ossining, NY

RECEIVED 9/11

43

Those who marry Dog Codependents can forget about their privacy.

Dear Dog Codependents Anonymous:

When I got married I broke my husband in properly. We picked up two stray dogs on our wedding night and snuck them into our hotel! We've been living and working for our own 'kids' since. We have two (so far): Max, an 8-year old Pit-Beagle mix and Gidget, a 9-year old goof (Doberman and Gods-knows-what mix)

Please add me to your mailing list.

B.T.
Katy, TX

RECEIVED 7/18

45

If you are involved with a Dog Codependent, you must be willing to help them cope with their weaknesses.

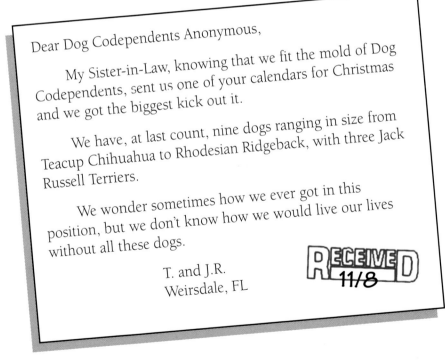

Dear Dog Codependents Anonymous,

My Sister-in-Law, knowing that we fit the mold of Dog Codependents, sent us one of your calendars for Christmas and we got the biggest kick out it.

We have, at last count, nine dogs ranging in size from Teacup Chihuahua to Rhodesian Ridgeback, with three Jack Russell Terriers.

We wonder sometimes how we ever got in this position, but we don't know how we would live our lives without all these dogs.

T. and J.R.
Weirsdale, FL

RECEIVED
11/8

47

Many people who fall in love with Dog Codependents end up becoming afflicted themselves.

Quotations to Live by:

It is a terrible thing for an old woman to outlive her dog.
Tennessee Williams

To call him a dog hardly seems to do him justice, though, inasmuch as he had four legs, a tail, and barked, I admit he was, to all outward appearances. But to those of us who knew him well, he was a perfect gentleman.
Herione Gingold

A door is what a dog is perpetually on the wrong side of.
Ogden Nash

Dog Codependents enjoy nothing more than spending a quiet evening with their "significant other".

Dear Dog People:

My favorite dog quote comes from a Valentine card I found in a drug store a few years ago. It says:

"Other and different loves will be yours in life.
Yours alone will be mine forever.

Dogs have hearts, too.
Happy Valentine's Day.

Your Best Friend."

Thank you for listening to my stories and for creating an organization for other people like me.

Sincerely,

M.D.C.
Tulsa, OK

RECEIVED
3/16

If you are dating a Dog Codependent, be prepared to spend many Sundays taking the dogs out to "get some air."

Dear Dog Codependents Anonymous,

Our Miniature Pincher, Rambo, is our baby. He rules the roost. If one of us accidently says "bye-bye," that person has to take him in the car around the block. The same thing happens if we have to go somewhere and he can't go.

Thanks,

C.S.
Fremont, CA

RECEIVED
7/22

Chapter 4

Financial Consequences of Dog Codependency

Dear Dog Codependents Anonymous,

I just discovered your calendar last year when my husband gave one to me for Christmas. We can relate to EVERYthing in it!!! We are such Dog Codependents!!! It all started in 1987 when we finally got a house and I was determined to finally have a dog. I informed my husband (K.) I was going down to the Humane Society to look over the dogs. He said he "didn't want no stinking furry mutt running around uncontrollably all over HIS house!!" and I would be totally responsible for it; he wanted NOTHING to do with it. Furthermore, this dog would not be allowed on the furniture, on the bed, or be given table scraps.

Guess what? Yep!!! He fell in love with the one dirty mutt I picked out (tho he wouldn't admit it for weeks). He insisted on naming him (Phineas), and yes, you guessed it, K. was the first one to encourage that dog to break every rule. In no time Phineas was sleeping between us, had claimed the large sofa as his, got his scraps of steak, etc... And we were buying all the best and most expensive food and toys and accessories there were. We took him to the vet for the slightest little thing, but would forego doctor visits for ourselves, being unable to justify spending that kind of money. Our vet bills were atrocious. Phineas was an adult Lhasa-Apso that had been abandoned. We had him cleaned up and groomed and he was the most gorgeous, smartest, most well behaved dog ever!!!

Then came Keisha. I knew Phineas's days were numbered and did a very dangerous thing...I ventured into a pet store. There she was...the most adorable little puppy ever! I fell in love; hurried home to tell K. what I wanted. Went back to the pet store. Oops! Learned she is a rare Japanese Chin purebred from champion lines, at a price tag of $800!!! K. said "NO." I promptly got out MY credit card and carried her home with me. Yes, she's as spoiled as any other. Now we have another Japanese Chin that we rescued from the "pound". I could tell endless dog stories.

K.M.
Mesa, AZ

RECEIVED
12/4

55

Some Dog Codependents spend more on clothes for their dogs than for themselves.

57

Dog Codependents must make sure their clothing matches the color of their dogs' fur, and will pay top dollar for clothes that won't show dog hair.

Top Ten Dog Names (U.S.)

1. Brandy
2. Lady
3. Max
4. Rocky
5. Sam
6. Heidi
7. Sheba
8. Ginger
9. Muffin
10. Bear

(Source: Cowing, The Complete Book of Pet Names, San Mateo: Fireplug Press, 1990)

Dog Codependents spend a fortune each year on shoes.

Dear Dog Codependents Anonymous,

I'm not alone! It is so nice to know there is help out there! I have one son, an 11-month old English Bulldog named Samson. I, like so many other Dog Codependents, would choose him over people any day. Surprisingly, my husband finds this hard to understand.

I never thought I would be fortunate enough to have the sweetest and most beautiful "child" on the planet. He is just like a real kid, only better (and probably cheaper —although not much!). When he looks up at me with those bulging eyes and wrinkled face after he just finished chewing up a pair of new shoes or a piece of furniture, the guilt in his eyes is so heartbreaking that rarely can I bring myself to discipline him.

Samson is not only beautiful and lovable, but he is also very creative. In obedience school he found new and unusual ways to disrupt the class on a weekly basis. He finally graduated—barely! I am worried that this rebellious spirit will cause a problem now that he is a teenager (he is about 15 in human years). I am considering putting him in counseling if I can afford it.

Thank you for your support.

A.V.
River Ridge, LA

61

Dog Codependents believe that it's their duty to feed every dog in the neighborhood...

Dear Dog Codependent Comrades,

My husband J. refers to me as the one "who feeds all the dogs in the neighborhood." We have a small dog, part Scottie and Cocker Spaniel. He is a real delight. We named him "Little Bit" because he was so small when we got him. Well, he's still small, but larger than we thought he'd be.

"Little Bit" started out as my dog, but now he's more J.'s than mine - they kinda compliment each other with their black hair and brown eyes.

L. and J.B.
Rose Hill, NC

RECEIVED
11/22

...which is why they must often buy their dog food in bulk.

Dear Dog Codependents Anonymous,

I have no problem publicly declaring that I get along with dogs better than most people. Our children are a 9-year old cocker/beagle mix and a 2-year old Cheaspeake Bay Retriever. My wife and I take them everywhere with us. They have more beds to sleep or sit on than we do, and that includes a twin bed which the two of them share during the day. In dog time, the Chessie has had more schooling than my wife and I combined. I think the wholesale pet supply store I use has my credit card number memorized. We truly are Dog Codependents, and it is nothing to be ashamed of. Nowhere can you find a more loyal friend than in a dog. My favorite part of the day, regardless of how it has gone, is to be welcomed with wagging tails, wet tongues and big smiles when I come home.

Please put us on your mailing list. Thanks for understanding.

Sincerely,

K. and R.H.
Tucker, GA

RECEIVED
1/18

For Dog Codependents, there is no such thing as a "naughty" dog, especially during the holidays.

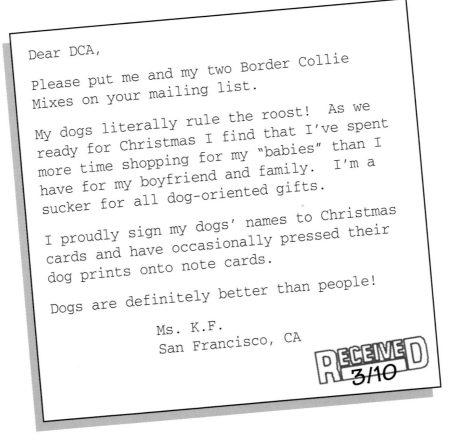

Dear DCA,

Please put me and my two Border Collie Mixes on your mailing list.

My dogs literally rule the roost! As we ready for Christmas I find that I've spent more time shopping for my "babies" than I have for my boyfriend and family. I'm a sucker for all dog-oriented gifts.

I proudly sign my dogs' names to Christmas cards and have occasionally pressed their dog prints onto note cards.

Dogs are definitely better than people!

Ms. K.F.
San Francisco, CA

RECEIVED
3/10

And when it comes to making doggie happy, Dog Codependents will spare no expense.

Dear Dog Codependents:

My husband gave me a miniature dachshund as a Christmas gift in 1990. She soon became the center of my life. I showered her with toys and dog treats and let her sleep with me in our bed. I even hand-knit afghans for the dog. My husband soon got into the act. For example, we were out at a pizza place with a group of friends during the time when they had some sort of promotion going where you could buy a basketball for $2 with each pizza order. While other "dads" purchased the balls for their sons and daughters, my husband had to buy one for his beloved Corky. It is still her favorite toy.

By August of 1991, my husband decided Corky needed a sister, so we adopted a second miniature wiener dog named Mitzi. Mitzi is the sweetest, happiest little dog and loves everyone—even cats!

Both dogs still sleep with us. When they are sick, one of us stays home from work with them (even though that means giving up precious vacation days). All guests who visit our home are required to throw slimy dog toys and play with the dogs or we will ask them to leave.

L.K.B.
Yakima, WA

RECEIVED 9/5

Serious Dog Codependents spend serious money at the vet and expect to be treated that way.

Dear Dog Codependents Anonymous,

I am graduating from Georgia Tech this year. My main goal is to graduate with good grades so I can provide my dog Hamlin with the kind of lifestyle he expects (and deserves…which is nothing but the best). I may even go on to graduate school to further secure Hamlin's future.

M.F.
Atlanta, GA

RECEIVED
7/21

Dog Codependents often have working relationships with their pets.

Dear Dog Codependents,

I am the owner of <u>Precious Pets Pet Sitting Service</u> in the Reading, PA area, since 1990. I have 2 German Shorthaired Pointers who are gracious enough to let me live with them. Besides myself, many of my clients are Dog-Codependents as well, so I can really relate!

G.Z.
Sinking Spring, PA

RECEIVED
7/25

When it comes to careers, a Dog Codependent's first concern isn't "How much will I make?" but rather, "Can I bring my dog to work with me."

Dear Dog Codependents Anonymous,

I have truly gone to the dogs. I was a registered nurse at our county hospital for 14 years, made good money and had excellent benefits. My love of animals—especially horses and dogs, was well known with my patients and fellow workers. Six years ago the position for manager of our Humane Society was available. Finally, a chance to work with animals!

I got the job and I'll be there til I die. I took a 50% cut in pay, have no health insurance, no retirement, and no pension plan. My parents are probably rolling over in their graves as I'm sure they didn't send me to college to clean kennels and cat cages! I'm poorer but happier—this is what I was put on this earth for!

D.L.
Iron Mountain, MI

RECEIVED
3/23

Chapter 5
Dog Codependent Families

Dear Dog Codependents,

I loved the calendar my daughter gave me, especially when I realized my human behavior fits into every month on the calendar. We have a year and a half old Chihuahua named "Baby." She is the answer to my mid-life crisis since, at 53 and after three grown children, there are no more pitter-patters of little feet in the house.

Baby not only eats dinner with us, (*dog food you say, God forbid!*) if we have something she dislikes, it's off to the grocery store for a 1/4 lb. of roast beef. She sleeps at our side (whomever she picks for the night) so closely you wonder how she can breathe. Baby is paper trained, which is picked up twice a day. Her little toes don't know what the pavement feels like. She's also bathed twice a week, by me, of course. She gets her nails cut every three weeks by a very well chosen groomer. They love to see her come in, they don't even charge me!

We don't take vacations anymore. For Memorial Day this year we went to the Hamptons. What a waste of time that was! I spent an additional $50.00 on phone calls to my daughter to see if Baby was eating, going to the bathroom, was upset, missed us, etc. So now we take day excursions, some of which we can take her on.

She accompanies us to the laundromat (ever fold clothes holding a Chihuahua? How about playing cards with a dog on your arm? I won, by the way!) You have to understand why we're like this — we are really normal people. But here is this little 3-lb. fawn-colored, short-haired, big-eyed, painted face piece of life that steals every heart she comes into contact with.

When we arrive home from work, you can hear her cries in the hallway downstairs. It takes her ten minutes to calm down, after we practically hug and kiss her to death. So tell me, how can you *not* be a "Dog Codependent" with something like this in your life?

Sincerely,

M.R.
Bronx, NY

RECEIVED
8/25

Birthdays are important occasions for Dog Codependent families.

Dog Codependents Anonymous,

As the mother of a Dog Codependent, in contemplating her upbringing as a good daughter, I have failed to see where I could have gone wrong. My daughter is the "mother" of a 3-year old German Short Haired Pointer, named Winnie. Winnie has not yet been told that she is a dog. She thinks that she is a person, and comports herself accordingly.

Each year her "mother" throws her a lavish SURPRISE birthday party, to which her dearest and nearest friends and relations are invited. Gifts are encouraged. Personally, I am on the hook for a large gift certificate. I always receive an acknowledgment from my daughter who states that "Winnie is so overwhelmed by the generous gift that she cannot speak and has asked me to convey her thanks."

At the first party two of Winnie's dog friends were invited, but after one lifted his leg on a sofa and the other pooped on the rug, they were crossed off the guest list.

Sincerely yours,

S.R.
Boca Raton, FL

78

At family reunions, Dog Codependents invariably end up showing off their dogs' talents.

Quotations to Live by:

If you pick up a starving dog and make him prosperous,
    he will not bite you.
This is the principal difference between a dog and a man.
     Mark Twain

If you want a true friend in Washington, get yourself a dog.
     Harry Truman

You ain't nothin' but a hound dog, cryin' all the time.
Well, you ain't never caught a rabbit and you ain't
    no friend of mine.
     Howard Lieber & Mike Stoller

81

When traveling, Dog Codependent families rely on the telephone to combat homesickness.

Dear Dog Codependents,

I am a self admitted Dog Codependent. You are probably the only people who could understand what it is like to not be able to function for an entire week because your dog died. It's good to be among friends. I took my current dog, Trisha, away from her very abusive people. I decided they were not good parents, and that she needed me (a VERY codependent thought). So, here I am making phone calls to a dog when I'm out of town, talking to her as if she can answer.

I have found myself, on a number of occasions, having a very heated argument with my dog. She usually wins because her bark is VERY big, and I'm really not interested in finding out about her bite. She is the consummate mutt, and for that we love her even more. As the saying goes, "The more people I know, the better I like my dog."

Sincerely,

L.J.E.
Everett, WA

RECEIVED 6/24

83

All Dog Codependent families enjoy including their pets in their holiday traditions.

Dear Dog Codependents Anonymous,

We have a 17 month Yellow Labrador named Sunny, who I truly want the whole world to know about because he means so much to us. We are trying to give him the best possible life. He is very well trained, walked and exercised daily. He enjoys swimming, canoeing, rafting and playing long hours with his puppy friends with whom he is extremely well socialized.

My husband thinks I need help! Sunny spends all his time going everywhere with us, including going to have pictures taken with Santa to make Christmas Cards. We decorate our tree with our collection of dog-bone ornaments. My husband also helped organize Sunny's first birthday party last July with MORE dogs than people. It was a blast! We can't wait til his 2nd.

S. and K.C.
Philadelphia, PA

RECEIVED
2/17

Dog Codependents make good use of their "family rooms."

Dog Codependents often include their dogs in their exercise routines.

Dog Codependents Anonymous,

Thank you, finally someone who understands me!
First of all, I have to admit that I will sleep with my
feet at the head of the bed just to get close enough to
my dog to have my arm around him and feel his hot
breath on my cheek.

As a Dog Codependent, my dog, Hickory, rules my
life. When he barks I get the afghan out so he can
snuggle under it on the couch. He is also my running
partner. He has helped me to train for many half
marathons and two full marathons. Do I need
therapy?

J.B.
Littleton, CO

RECEIVED
4/28

89

Housekeeping can be especially challenging for Dog Codependent households.

Fellow Dog Codependents,

As my husband and I found ourselves working more and more hours, we decided we needed to get Brittany, our Dalmatian, a companion to keep her company on those long days that she had to stay home alone.

Then in comes Mickey. We brought him home when he was just 4 weeks old and I fell instantly in love with this beautiful, blue eyed puppy. Each and every morning Mickey would curl up around my neck and want to be hugged and cuddled. Well, as the months went by that adorable little puppy grew and grew and grew! He still has his blue eyes but his cuteness slowly began to fade. The curtains that once hung from my patio door are now shreds of cloth. My nice white walls now have plaster patches all over them. I don't have one corner of carpeting that has padding underneath it and my new loveseat is down to bare wood along the base.

Brittany's companion turned out to be our worst nightmare! But through all of this he has turned out to be my "best friend." He welcomes me home like no one else could. He still cuddles and nuzzles with me every morning and he is the best electric blanket on a cold wintery night.

I guess I can always buy new curtains. I can always replace the pads under my carpets and I still have plenty of plaster patch left under my sink. But nothing in this world could replace the love I get from Mickey day after day.

A.C.
Mentor, OH

RECEIVED
4/22

91

Chapter 6

Managing your Dog Codependency

Dear Dog Codependents,

I have four poodles - one toy, one miniature and two standards - they let me share their house with them.

Why is it that I never have enough money to get my own hair cut, but they are groomed every 6 to 8 weeks? And I tend to stay clear of doctors while at least one of my dogs is at the vet's once a month. Does this qualify me as a Dog Codependent?

One of the standards, 4-year old "Barney," was born in Cape Elizabeth, Maine and is a real **"Maineiac"**. He's 75 pounds of pure Yankee stubbornness. He rules the house and thinks of me as a subordinate litter mate until I have to set him straight. Due to his size he may be the alpha dog to the other dogs in the family, but not to me. Growling works wonders when you know how to do it. I wear him down eventually and he backs off.

I could go on but I won't.

                              B.J.W.
                              Salisbury, MA

While you may never be entirely cured of your Dog Codependency, you can certainly gain control of your condition. The first step is to admit to yourself once and for all that your life is controlled by canines.

Dear Dog Codependents Anonymous,

I just received your calendar and I was truly amazed that there are other dog crazy folks out there besides me.

I'll take dogs over humans any day. I am proud to be owned by eight dogs, ranging in size from a 20-lb. Cockapoo to a 190-lb. Irish Wolfhound.

My dogs are my best friends and the loves of my life.

J.S.
Hayes, VA

RECEIVED
10/8

There are many different variations of Dog Codependency. Take a good, honest look at yourself and figure out which one applies to you. This will make treatment much easier.

Stop trying to hide your "habit."
You're not fooling anyone but yourself.

Dear Dog Codependents!

A very dear friend gave me your calendar for Christmas. I love it! I have snuck doggies into motels and hotels all over the country.

Yes, I am hooked for life. "Bonkers" has been running this house and me for 7 years. Before that it was "Rebel," then "Toddy" and "Copper"...get the picture?

What wonderful friends!

Codependently yours,

B.L.

RECEIVED
2/18

99

Focus on slowly breaking your old patterns. If you are one of those Dog Codependents who obsessively bathes your pet, let a day or two go by without washing your doggie. Slowly increase the time between baths until you are only bathing your dog every year or two like most dog owners.

Get a life. Rather than spend another fruitless night trying to teach your old dog new tricks, get out of the house. Go see a play or a film _without the dog_ (Your dog will appreciate the break).

103

To free yourself from the Dog Codependency that binds you, you must also change your environment. Stop frequenting the places where other Dog Codependents congregate.

Dear DCA,

My daughter got married and we got a puppy! Nikki has totally consumed our lives. Instead of sleeping late on the weekends, we go to a park and meet 10 other Codependents with their "babies" at 9:00 am every Sat. and Sun. (rain, snow or shine) so that the dogs can get exercise!

Although we all clean up after our "babies," the park eventually put up a sign saying "leash your dogs." Well, we came in the middle of the night and, miraculously, the sign "disappeared."

Do I qualify?

S.H.
Ft. Washington, PA

Create a new circle of friends.
Introduce them to your pet if you must,
but remember that they may not
appreciate your dog, or forgive his
shortcomings, the way you do.

Quotations to Live by:

The greatest pleasure of a dog is that you may make a fool of
yourself with him and not only will he not scold you, but he will
make a fool of himself, too.
Samuel Butler

Dogs' lives are too short, which is their only fault, really.
Agnes Turnbull

The poor dog, in life the firmest friend,
The first to welcome, foremost to defend.
Lord Byron

While learning to cope with your Dog Codependency, don't take yourself too seriously. Take time to have some fun. Laughter really is one of the best medicines.

Dear Fellow Dog Lovers,

We have a Lhasa Apso. He is **so** funny. He has a thousand faces, especially after he eats. His dinner gets all over him. We call him "Bud."

C.S.
San Jacinto, CA

RECEIVED
6/28

As you and your dog slowly untangle your relationship, you will both become freer to appreciate and love each other for who you really are without limiting or threatening each other's individuality or independence.

During this process you will find, as many other Dog Codependents before you have found, your relationship with your pet blossoming and growing into something more wonderful than you ever imagined possible.

You will never be totally cured of your Dog Codependency, but let's face it, you wouldn't really want to be totally cured, would you?

About the Author

Ronnie Sellers was born and raised in Philadelphia. He graduated from the University of Pennsylvania, where he was awarded the Phi Kappa Sigma Fellowship Award for prose.

He has written for radio, film and television and has authored three children's books, *If Christmas Were A Poem, When Springtime Comes* and *My First Day At School*, as well as *The Official Cat Codependents Handbook*.

In 1976 Ronnie was a co-founder of Renaissance Greeting Cards, where he created greeting cards for twelve years. In 1991 he formed his own publishing and licensing company, Ronnie Sellers Productions.

Ronnie has four children and lives and works in Kennebunk, ME.

About the Artist

Jennifer Black Reinhardt grew up in Hollidaysburg, PA and graduated from Carnegie Mellon University with a degree in Illustration. She is the creator of her own line of humorous greeting cards and was cited for her exceptional card design by the National Greeting Card Association in 1991.

Jennifer's work has been featured in several publications, including *The Artist's Market, The Best Contemporary Women's Humor,* and *The Complete Guide to Greeting Card Design and Illustration.*

She has recently written and illustrated her first children's book, *The Giant's Toybox,* and illustrated *The Official Cat Codependents Handbook.* She is also very happy to be illustrating *The Official Cat Codependents Calendar* and *The Official Dog Codependents Calendar,* both published by Ronnie Sellers Productions.